Take a look at (TALAT 30)

Each of us has a 'Life Profile' of who we are,
what we do, how we do it and what it means to us.

Each of us builds our own unique,
capacities, capabilities & competences
to create our own 'LifeTime'

HomiGenesis

Ecclesiast
Hominist
TechnoPreneur
Originateur
Individuateur
Communicateur
PrintMediateur

Take a look at (TALAT 30) _ PRINT 2018 - Chicago

A PrintWorld of Opportunity

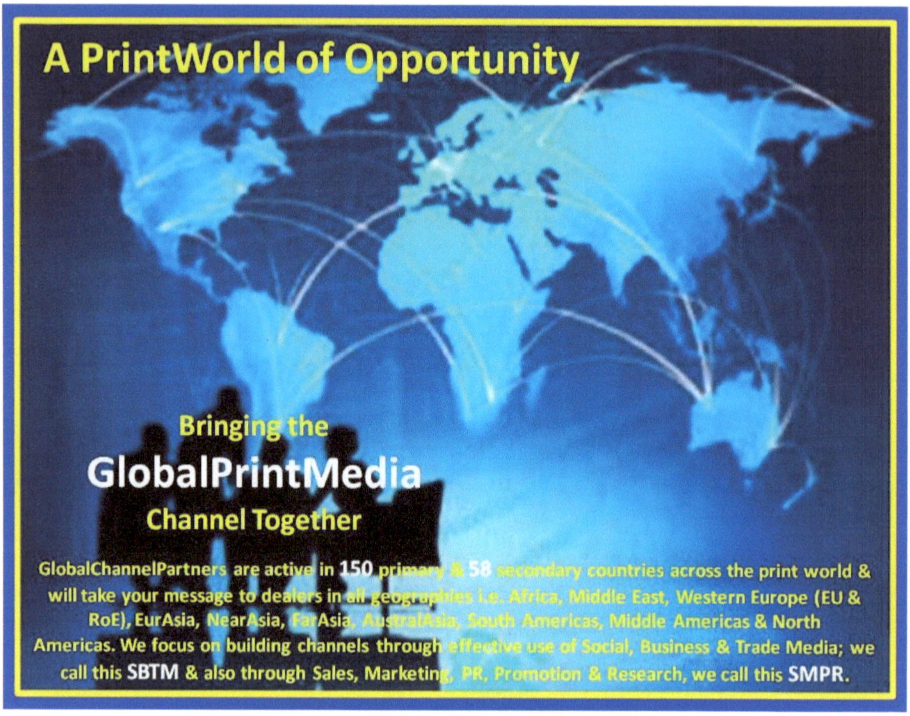

A PrintWorld of Opportunity

Bringing the GlobalPrintMedia Channel Together

GlobalChannelPartners are active in **150** primary & **58** secondary countries across the print world & will take your message to dealers in all geographies i.e. Africa, Middle East, Western Europe (EU & RoE), EurAsia, NearAsia, FarAsia, AustralAsia, South Americas, Middle Americas & North Americas. We focus on building channels through effective use of Social, Business & Trade Media; we call this **SBTM** & also through Sales, Marketing, PR, Promotion & Research, we call this **SMPR**.

Take a look at (TALAT 30) _ A PRINTWorld of Op[opportunity

GlobalChannelPartners - PrintMediator - PrintMediateur - PrintMediaPartners

GlobalChannelPartners working with Manufacturers, Distributors, Dealers, Print Consultants, Print Media (Online & Offline) Print Event & Exhibition Organisers, Print Associations, Major & Trade Printers, Major & Trade Packagers, Major & Trade Creatives, major & Trader Publishers, Education, Academic & Research Institutions in North America, Caribbean & Central America, South America, Europe EU, Europe RoE, Africa, Middle East, Near Asia (incl India), Far Asia (incl China, Japan & Korea) & Austral Asia.

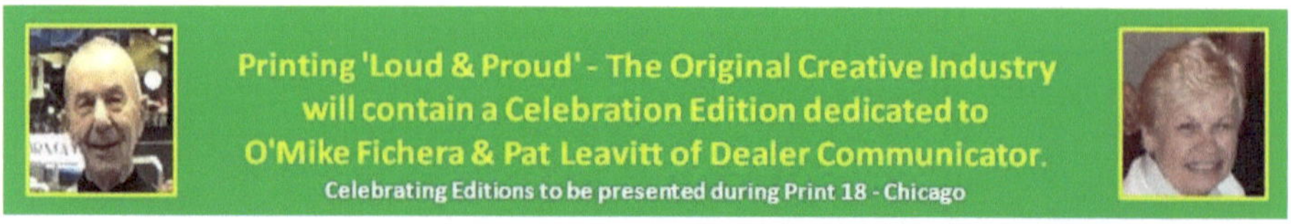

Printing 'Loud & Proud' - The Original Creative Industry will contain a Celebration Edition dedicated to O'Mike Fichera & Pat Leavitt of Dealer Communicator. Celebrating Editions to be presented during Print 18 - Chicago

Printing – The Original Creative Industry – dedicated to Mike Fichera & Pat Leavitt

Take a look at (TALAT 30 GlobalChannelPartners - PrintMediator - PrintMediateur - PrintMediaPartners

Take a look at (TALAT 30) _ PrintMediateur Library

Take A Closer Look……(TALAT 30)

Takes a closer look at Ireland, Peru, Ghana, Indonesia, Turkey, Mexico, Egypt, Japan, Brazil, Greece, China, Chile, Norway, South Africa, Pakistan, Australia, Nigeria, Cuba, Vietnam, Italy, New Zealand, Saudi Arabia, South Korea, Spain, Canada, Poland, Thailand, France, Algeria & Bolivia provides an insight into these countries for printmedia manufacturers who are looking to extend their reach across the PRINTWorld.

Each has a 'Order Market Report' and a 'Plan a Campaign' opportunity.

Take a closer look at Ireland

Take a look at (TALAT 30) Ireland

A diversified print economy with a broad range of printing, packaging, creative and publishing companies served by well established and knowledgeable dealer partners. The economy of Ireland is a knowledge economy, focused on services into high-tech, life sciences and financial services industries. Ireland is an open economy, and ranks first for high-value FDI flows. Wikipedia

Population: 4.68m

Currency: Euro   Capital: Dublin

Gross domestic product: 294.1 billion USD (2016) World Bank

Unemployment rate: 6.1% (Mar 2018) Eurostat

GDP per capita: 61,606.48 USD (2016) World Bank

Government debt: 72.8% of GDP (2016) Eurostat

Minimum wage: 1,613.95 EUR per month (Jan 2018) Eurostat

GDP growth rate: 5.2% annual change (2016) World Bank

Take a closer look at Peru

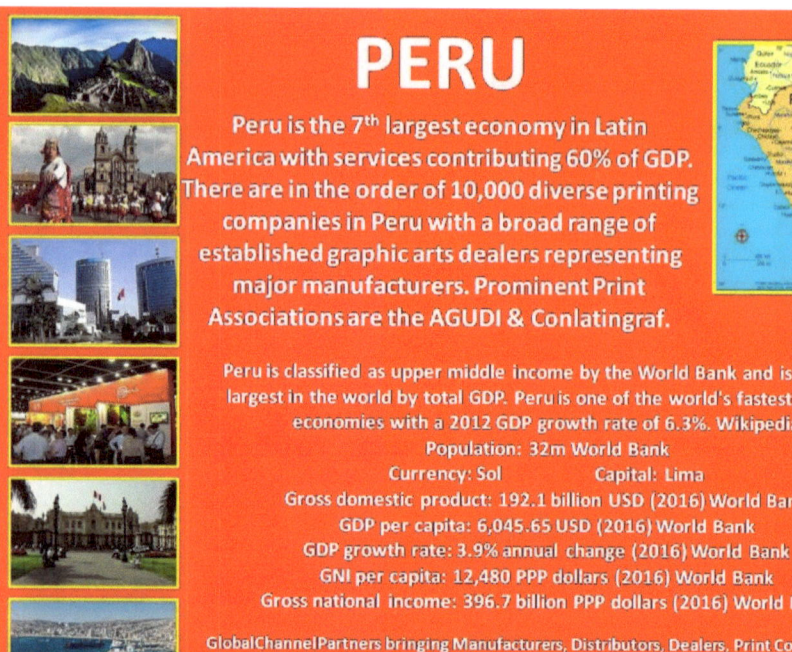

Take a look at (TALAT 30) Peru

Peru is the 7th largest economy in Latin America with services contributing 60% of GDP. There are in the order of 10,000 diverse printing companies in Peru with a broad range of established graphic arts dealers representing major manufacturers. Prominent Print Associations are the AGUDI & Conlatingraf.

Peru is classified as upper middle income by the World Bank and is the 39th largest in the world by total GDP. Peru is one of the world's fastest-growing economies with a 2012 GDP growth rate of 6.3%. Wikipedia

Population: 32m World Bank

Currency: Sol   Capital: Lima

Gross domestic product: 192.1 billion USD (2016) World Bank

GDP per capita: 6,045.65 USD (2016) World Bank

GDP growth rate: 3.9% annual change (2016) World Bank

GNI per capita: 12,480 PPP dollars (2016) World Bank

Gross national income: 396.7 billion PPP dollars (2016) World Bank

Take a closer look at Ghana

Take a look at (TALAT 30) Ghana

About 95% of Ghanaian printers are situated in and around Kumasi and Accra. The total number of Publishing and Printing houses is in the order of 502 with 102 being Publishing and 400 being Printing houses. There are both local indigenous and supra regional dealers. The GPPCA is a significant print trade association in Ghana.

The economy of Ghana has a diverse and rich resource base, including the manufacturing and exportation of digital technology goods, automotive and ship construction and exportation, and the exportation ...Wikipedia

Currency: Ghanaian cedi   Capital: Accra
Gross domestic product: 42.69 billion USD (2016) World Bank
GDP per capita: 1,513.46 USD (2016) World Bank
GNI per capita: 4,150 PPP dollars (2016) World Bank
GDP growth rate: 3.6% annual change (2016) World Bank
Gross national income: 117.2 billion PPP dollars (2016) World Bank
Internet users: 14.1% of the population (2011) World Bank

Take a closer look at Indonesia

Indonesia

There are in the order of 14,000 Printers in Indonesia. International manufacturers are well represented by a number of Graphic Arts Suppliers. The Indonesian Graphic Arts Industry is growing faster than the Global Average. The Population stands at 266+ m (3.5% of the Global Total) and is growing rapidly. The Major Trade Association is : Indonesia Master Printers Association: PPGI. Major Trade Show : AllPrintIndonesia

Upcoming
Turkey - Mexico - Egypt

Indonesia has the largest economy in Southeast Asia and is one of the emerging market economies of the world. The country is also a member of G-20 major economies and classified as a newly industrialized country. Wikipedia
Currency: Indonesian rupiah   Capital: Jakarta
Gross domestic product: 932.3 billion USD (2016) World Bank
GDP per capita: 3,570.29 USD (2016) World Bank
GDP growth rate: 5.0% annual change (2016) World Bank
GNI per capita: 11,220 PPP dollars (2016) World Bank
Gross national income: 2.929 trillion PPP dollars (2016) World Bank
Internet users: 18.0% of the population (2011) World Bank

GlobalChannelPartners bringing Manufacturers, Distributors, Dealers, Print Consultants, Print Associations, Print Media (Offline & Online) Print Event & Exhibition Organisers, Major & Trade Printers, Major & Trade Packagers, Major & Trade Creatives, Major & Trade Publishers, Education, Academic & Research Institutions working in the GlobalPrintEconomy.

Take a look at (TALAT 30) Indonesia

There are in the order of 14,000 Printers in Indonesia. International manufacturers are well represented by a number of Graphic Arts Suppliers. The Indonesian Graphic Arts Industry is growing faster than the Global Average. The Population stands at 266+ m (3.5% of the Global Total) and is growing rapidly. The Major Trade Association is : Indonesia Master Printers Association: PPGI. Major Trade Show: AllPrintIndonesia. Indonesia has the largest economy in Southeast Asia and is one of the emerging market economies of the world. The country is also a member of G-20 major economies and classified as a newly industrialized country. Wikipedia

Currency: Indonesian rupiah   Capital: Jakarta
Gross domestic product: 932.3 billion USD (2016) World Bank
GDP per capita: 3,570.29 USD (2016) World Bank
GDP growth rate: 5.0% annual change (2016) World Bank
GNI per capita: 11,220 PPP dollars (2016) World Bank
Gross national income: 2.929 trillion PPP dollars (2016) World Bank
Internet users: 18.0% of the population (2011) World Bank

Take a closer look at Turkey

Take a look at (TALAT 30) Turkey

A uniquely transcontinental country and culture which connects Europe with Asia and has a vibrant and diverse printing industry. Global manufacturers such as CETA & Avalon are well served by a broad range of excellent dealer partners. Istanbul is the major print centre. Major Trade Association: Basev. Major Trade Publication: Matbaa & Teknik. Major Trade Show: Printtek

The economy of Turkey is defined as an emerging market economy by the IMF. Turkey is among the world's developed countries according to the CIA World Factbook. Wikipedia. Currency: Turkish lira   Capital: Istanbul Population: 80m

Gross domestic product: 857.7 billion USD (2016) World Bank

GDP per capita: 10,787.61 USD (2016) World Bank

Government debt: 42.4% of GDP (2010) Eurostat

Minimum wage: 446.40 EUR per month (Jan 2018) Eurostat

GDP growth rate: 2.9% annual change (2016) World Bank

Unemployment rate: 9.9% (Dec 2017) Eurostat

Take a closer look at Mexico

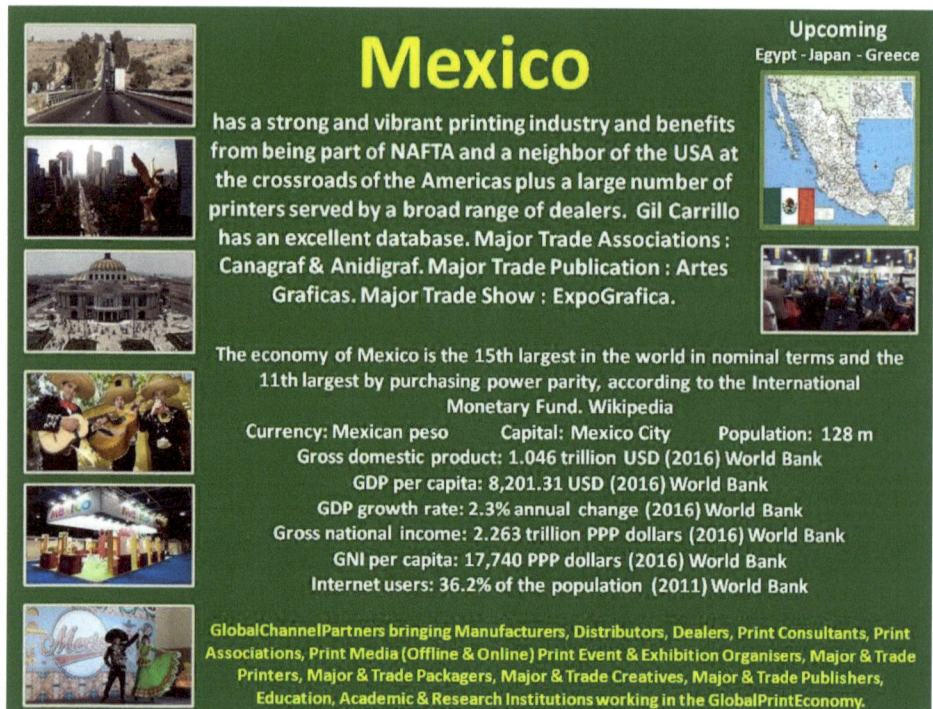

Take a look at (TALAT 30) Mexico

Mexico has a strong and vibrant printing industry and benefits from being part of NAFTA and a neighbor of the USA at the crossroads of the Americas plus a large number of printers served by a broad range of dealers. Gil Carrillo has an excellent database. Major Trade Associations: Canagraf & Anidigraf. Major Trade Publication: Artes Graficas. Major Trade Show: ExpoGrafica.

The economy of Mexico is the 15th largest in the world in nominal terms and the 11th largest by purchasing power parity, according to the IMF.

Currency: Mexican peso   Capital: Mexico City   Population: 128 m

Gross domestic product: 1.046 trillion USD (2016) World Bank

GDP per capita: 8,201.31 USD (2016) World Bank

GDP growth rate: 2.3% annual change (2016) World Bank

Gross national income: 2.263 trillion PPP dollars (2016) World Bank

GNI per capita: 17,740 PPP dollars (2016) World Bank

Internet users: 36.2% of the population (2011) World Bank

Take a closer look at Egypt

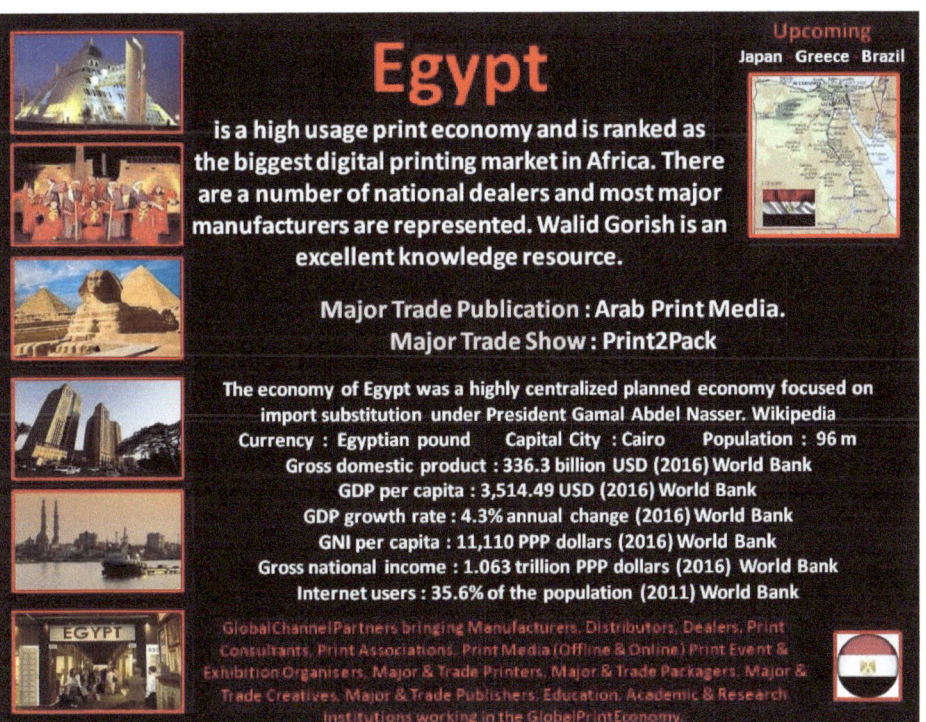

Take a look at (TALAT 30) Egypt

Egypt is a high usage print economy and is ranked as the biggest digital printing market in Africa. There are a number of national dealers and most major manufacturers are represented. Walid Gorish is an excellent knowledge resource.

The economy of Egypt was a highly centralized planned economy focused on import substitution under President Gamal Abdel Nasser. Wikipedia

Currency : Egyptian pound   Capital City : Cairo   Population: 96 m

Gross domestic product: 336.3 billion USD (2016) World Bank

GDP per capita: 3,514.49 USD (2016) World Bank

GDP growth rate: 4.3% annual change (2016) World Bank

GNI per capita : 11,110 PPP dollars (2016) World Bank

Gross national income : 1.063 trillion PPP dollars (2016) World Bank

Internet users : 35.6% of the population (2011) World Bank

Take a closer look at Japan

Japan

Upcoming
Greece - Brazil - China

There are 30,000+ printers in one of our globally leading manufacturer and innovator countries. Home of Fuji, Konica - Minolta, Komori, Canon, Duplo, Sakurai, Toray, Uchida and many others.

Major Trade Associations : JFPI & JPMA   Major Trade Show : IGAS

The economy of Japan is a highly developed & market-oriented economy. It is the third-largest in the world by nominal GDP & the fourth-largest by purchasing power, the world's 2nd largest developed economy. Wikipedia
Currency: Japanese yen   **Capital :** Tokyo   **Population :** 130 m
Gross domestic product: 4.939 trillion USD (2016) World Bank
GDP per capita: 38,894.47 USD (2016) World Bank
Gross national income: 5.444 trillion PPP dollars (2016) World Bank
GNI per capita: 42,870 PPP dollars (2016) World Bank
Internet users : 78.7% of the population (2011) World Bank

GlobalChannelPartners bringing Manufacturers, Distributors, Dealers, Print Consultants, Print Associations, Print Media (Offline & Online) Print Event & Exhibition Organisers, Major & Trade Printers, Major & Trade Packagers, Major & Trade Creatives, Major & Trade Publishers, Education, Academic & Research Institutions working in the GlobalPrintEconomy.

Take a look at (TALAT 30) Japan

There are 30,000+ printers in one of our globally leading manufacturer and innovator countries. Home of Fuji, Konica - Minolta, Komori, Canon, Duplo, Sakurai, Toray, Uchida and many others.

Major Trade Associations: JFPI & JPMA   Major Trade Show : IGAS
The economy of Japan is a highly developed & market-oriented economy. It is the third-largest in the world by nominal GDP & the fourth-largest by purchasing power, the world's 2nd largest developed economy. Wikipedia
Currency: Japanese yen   Capital: Tokyo   Population: 130 m
Gross domestic product: 4.939 trillion USD (2016) World Bank
GDP per capita: 38,894.47 USD (2016) World Bank
Gross national income: 5.444 trillion PPP dollars (2016) World Bank
GNI per capita: 42,870 PPP dollars (2016) World Bank
Internet users : 78.7% of the population (2011) World Bank

Take a closer look at Brazil

Take a look at (TALAT 30) Brazil

Brazil there are 20,000+ printers in one of our largest indigenous printing industries, a central access point to the South American market of 60,000+ printers. A principal market for Germany, the USA & China. IBF a well known example of a global channel partner. Major Trade Association: ABIGRAF   Major Trade Show: ExpoPrint

The economy of Brazil is the world's eighth largest economy by nominal GDP & eighth largest by purchasing power parity. The Brazilian economy is characterized by a mixed economy that relies on import substitution to achieve economic growth.

Currency: Brazilian real Trending   Capital: Brasilia   Population : 201 m

Gross domestic product: 1.796 trillion USD (2016) World Bank

GDP per capita: 8,649.95 USD (2016) World Bank

GDP growth rate: -3.6% annual change (2016) World Bank

GNI per capita: 14,810 PPP dollars (2016) World Bank

Gross national income: 3.075 trillion PPP dollars (2016) World Bank

Internet users: 45.0% of the population (2011) World Bank

Take a closer look at Greece

Take a look at (TALAT 30) Greece

Greece a broad and versatile industry with beautiful 6,000 islands with many great printing & packaging companies. Logistically, a great access point to the Balkans and a southern entry point into Europe. Kladis is a well known global channel partner. Major Trade Association : HFPMC Major Trade Show:Graphica Expo

The economy of Greece is the 48th largest in the world with a nominal gross domestic product of $192.691 billion per annum. It is also the 55th largest in the world by purchasing power parity at $288.418 billion per annum. Wikipedia

Currency: Euro   Capital: Athens   Population: 11 m
Government debt: 180.8% of GDP (2016)   Eurostat
Gross domestic product: 194.6 billion USD (2016) World Bank
Unemployment rate: 20.8% (Nov 2017) Eurostat
GDP per capital: 18,103.97 USD (2016) World Bank
GDP growth rate: 0.0% annual change (2016) World Bank
Minimum wage: 683.76 EUR per month (Jan 2018) Eurostat

Take a closer look at China

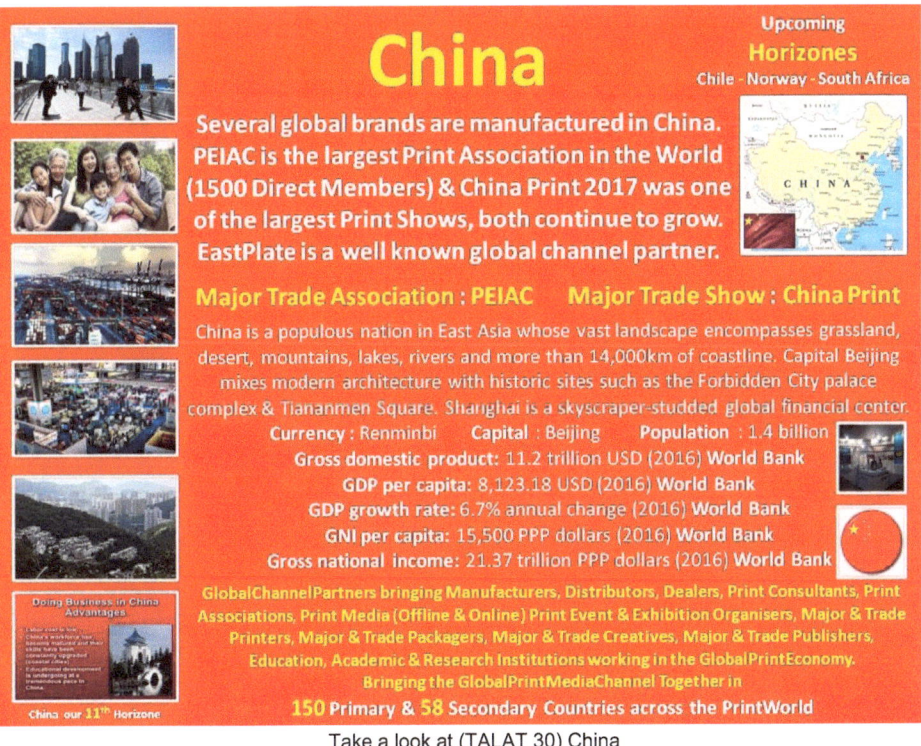

Take a look at (TALAT 30) China

China several global brands are manufactured in China. PEIAC is the largest Print Association in the World (1500 Direct Members) & China Print 2017 was one of the largest Print Shows, both continue to grow. EastPlate is a well known global channel partner.

Major Trade Association: PEIAC Major Trade Show: China Print
China is a populous nation in East Asia whose vast landscape encompasses grassland, desert, mountains, lakes, rivers and more than 14,000km of coastline. Capital Beijing mixes modern architecture with historic sites such as the Forbidden City palace complex & Tiananmen Square. Shanghai is a skyscraper-studded global financial center.

Currency: Renminbi   Capital: Beijing   Population: 1.4 billion
Gross domestic product: 11.2 trillion USD (2016) World Bank
GDP per capita: 8,123.18 USD (2016) World Bank

Take a closer look at Chile

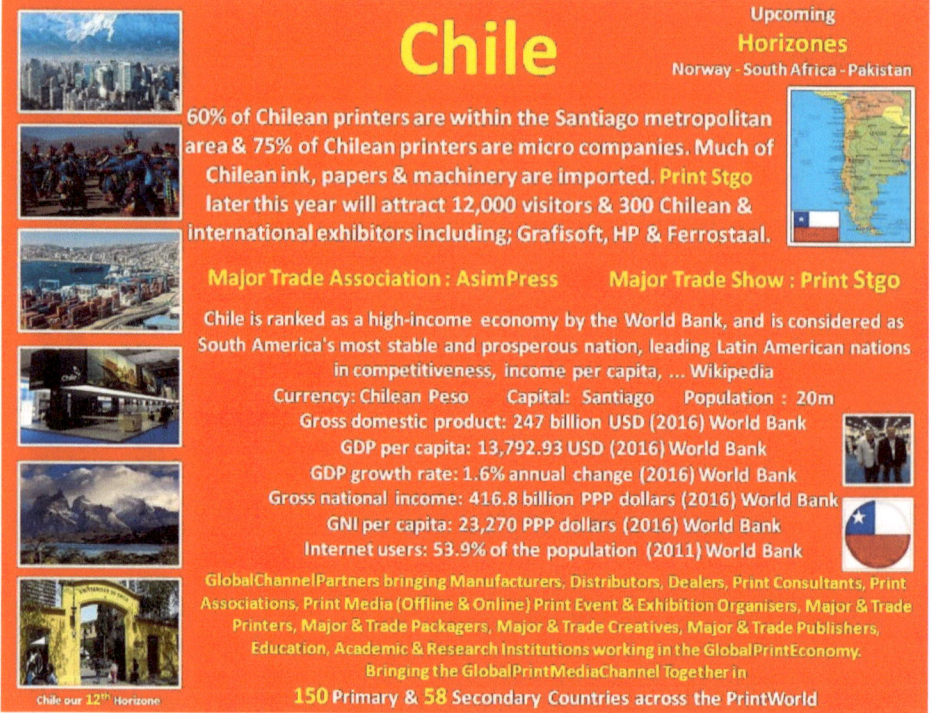

Take a look at (TALAT 30) Chile

Chile 60% of Chilean printers are within the Santiago metropolitan area & 75% of Chilean printers are micro companies. Much of Chilean ink, papers & machinery are imported. Print Stgo later this year will attract 12,000 visitors & 300 Chilean & international exhibitors including; Grafisoft, HP & Ferrostaal.

Major Trade Association: AsimPress   Major Trade Show: Print Stgo

Chile is ranked as a high-income economy by the World Bank, and is considered as South America's most stable and prosperous nation, leading Latin American nations in competitiveness, income per capita, Wikipedia

Currency: Chilean Peso   Capital: Santiago   Population: 20m

Gross domestic product: 247 billion USD (2016) World Bank

GDP per capita: 13,792.93 USD (2016) World Bank

GDP growth rate: 1.6% annual change (2016) World Bank

Gross national income: 416.8 billion PPP dollars (2016) World Bank

GNI per capita: 23,270 PPP dollars (2016) World Bank

Internet users: 53.9% of the population (2011) World Bank

Take a closer look at Norway

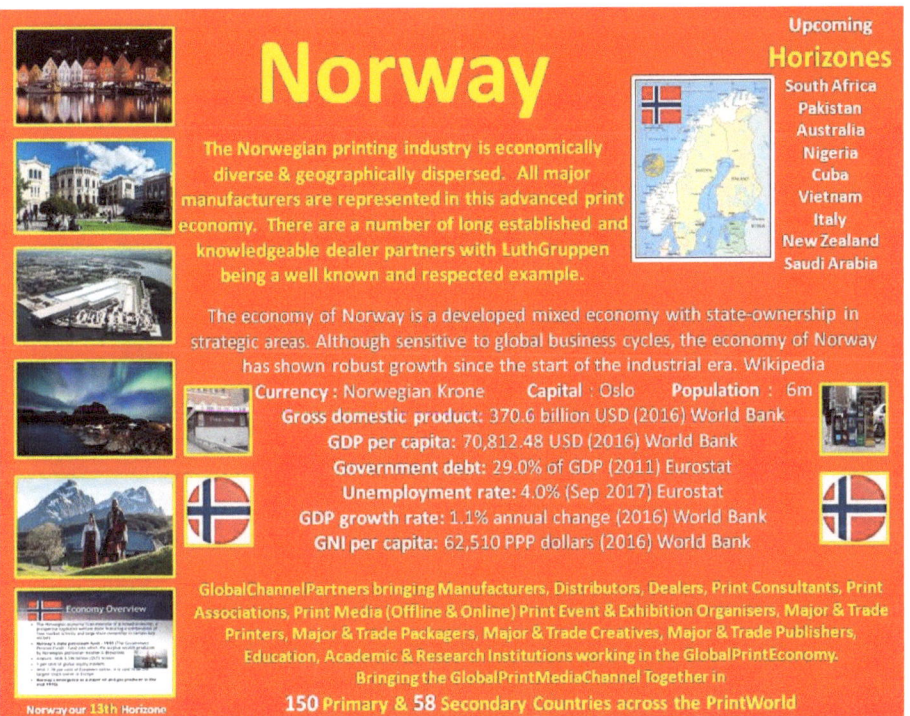

Take a look at (TALAT 30) Norway

The Norwegian printing industry is economically diverse & geographically dispersed. All major manufacturers are represented in this advanced print economy. There are a number of long established and knowledgeable dealer partners with LuthGruppen being a well known and respected example.

The economy of Norway is a developed mixed economy with state-ownership in strategic areas. Although sensitive to global business cycles, the economy of Norway has shown robust growth since the start of the industrial era. Wikipedia

Currency: Norwegian Krone   Capital: Oslo   Population: 6m

Gross domestic product: 370.6 billion USD (2016) World Bank

GDP per capita: 70,812.48 USD (2016) World Bank

Government debt: 29.0% of GDP (2011) Eurostat

Unemployment rate: 4.0% (Sep 2017) Eurostat

GDP growth rate: 1.1% annual change (2016) World Bank

GNI per capita: 62,510 PPP dollars (2016) World Bank

Take a closer look at South Africa

Take a look at (TALAT 30) South Africa

South Africa is the largest print production community on the continent & an ideal market access for the Southern African Region which includes Lesotho, Swaziland, Namibia, Botswana, Zimbabwe, Mozambique, Angola, Zambia, Tanzania, Comoros, Madagascar & Mauritius. Major Trade Association: PIFSA   Major Trade Show: Africa Print Expo .South Africa is a country on the southernmost tip of the African continent, marked by several distinct ecosystems. Inland safari destination Kruger National Park is populated by big game. The Western Cape offers beaches, lush wine lands around Stellenbosch & Paarl, craggy cliffs at the Cape of Good Hope, forest and lagoons along the Garden Route, the city of Cape Town, beneath flat-topped Table Mountain. Currency: South African rand   Capital: Cape Town Population: 56m

Gross domestic product: 294.8 billion USD (2016) World Bank

GDP per capita: 5,273.59 USD (2016) World Bank

GDP growth rate: 0.3% annual change (2016) World Bank

GNI per capita: 12,860 PPP dollars (2016) World Bank

Gross national income: 718.9 billion PPP dollars (2016) World Bank

Take a closer look at Pakistan

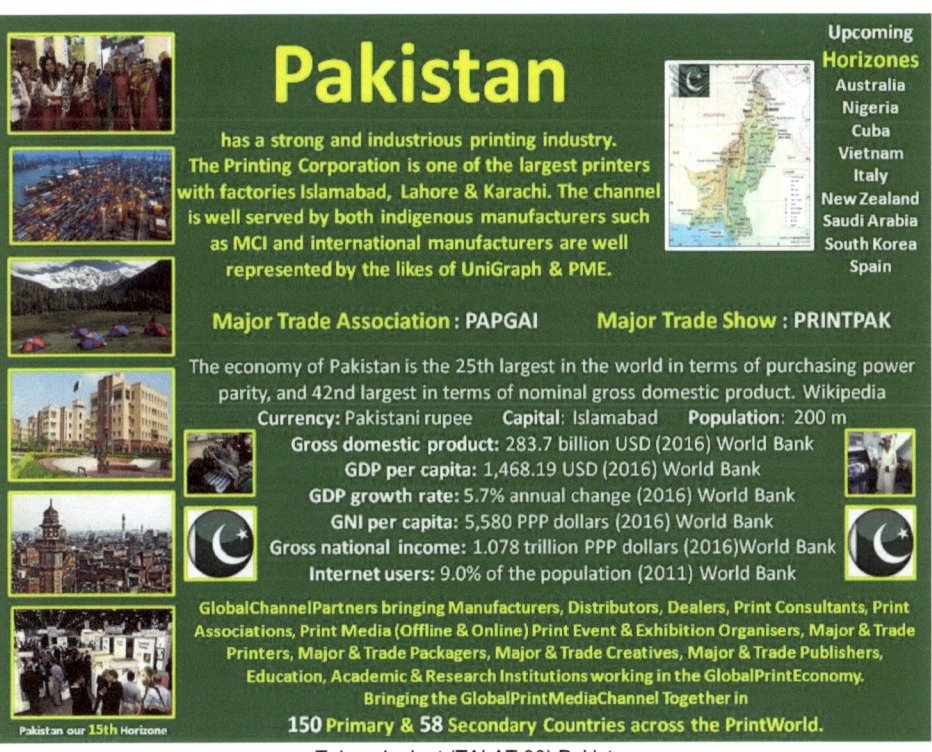

Take a look at (TALAT 30) Pakistan

Pakistan has a strong and industrious printing industry. The Printing Corporation is one of the largest printers with factories Islamabad, Lahore & Karachi. The channel is well served by both indigenous manufacturers such as MCI and international manufacturers are well represented by the likes of UniGraph & PME.

Major Trade Association: PAPGAI   Major Trade Show: PRINTPAK

The economy of Pakistan is the 25th largest in the world in terms of purchasing power parity, and 42nd largest in terms of nominal gross domestic product.

Currency: Pakistani rupee   Capital: Islamabad   Population: 200 m
Gross domestic product: 283.7 billion USD (2016) World Bank
GDP per capita: 1,468.19 USD (2016) World Bank
GDP growth rate: 5.7% annual change (2016) World Bank
GNI per capita: 5,580 PPP dollars (2016) World Bank
Gross national income: 1.078 trillion PPP dollars (2016) World Bank
Internet users: 9.0% of the population (2011) World Bank

Take a closer look at Australia

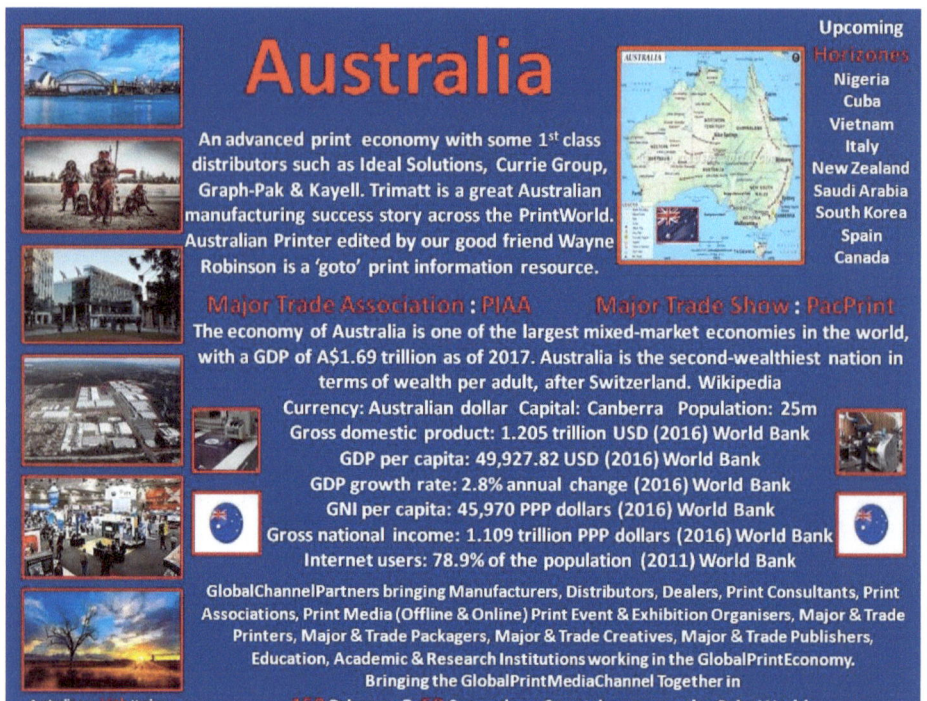

Take a look at (TALAT 30) Australia

Australia an advanced print economy with some 1st class distributors such as Ideal Solutions, Currie Group, Graph-Pak & Kayell. Trimatt is a great Australian manufacturing success story across the PrintWorld. Australian Printer edited by our good friend Wayne Robinson is a 'goto' print information resource.

Major Trade Association: PIAA   Major Trade Show: PacPrint

The economy of Australia is one of the largest mixed-market economies in the world, with a GDP of A$1.69 trillion as of 2017. Australia is the second-wealthiest nation in terms of wealth per adult, after Switzerland. Wikipedia

Currency: Australian dollar   Capital: Canberra   Population: 25m

Gross domestic product: 1.205 trillion USD (2016) World Bank

GDP per capita: 49,927.82 USD (2016) World Bank

GDP growth rate: 2.8% annual change (2016) World Bank

GNI per capita: 45,970 PPP dollars (2016) World Bank

Gross national income: 1.109 trillion PPP dollars (2016) World Bank

Internet users: 78.9% of the population (2011) World Bank

Take a closer look at Nigeria

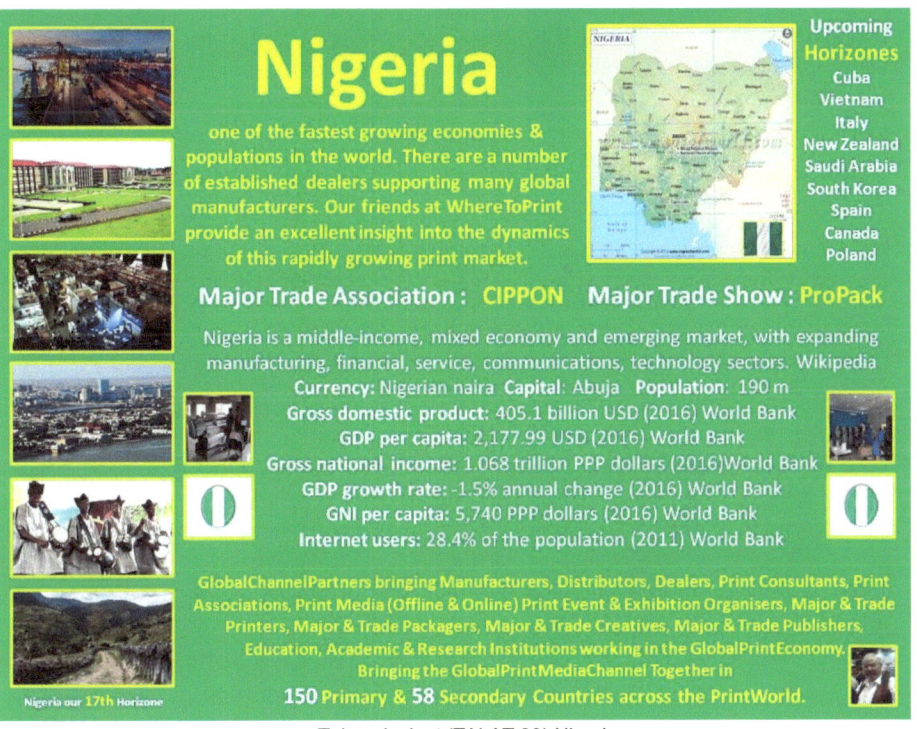

Take a look at (TALAT 30) Nigeria

Nigeria one of the fastest growing economies & populations in the world. There are a number of established dealers supporting many global manufacturers. Our friends at WhereToPrint provide an excellent insight into the dynamics of this rapidly growing print market.

Major Trade Association: CIPPON   Major Trade Show: ProPack

Nigeria is a middle-income, mixed economy and emerging market, with expanding manufacturing, financial, service, communications, and technology sectors.

Currency: Nigerian naira   Capital: Abuja   Population: 190 m

Gross domestic product: 405.1 billion USD (2016) World Bank

GDP per capita: 2,177.99 USD (2016) World Bank

Gross national income: 1.068 trillion PPP dollars (2016) World Bank

GDP growth rate: -1.5% annual change (2016) World Bank

GNI per capita: 5,740 PPP dollars (2016) World Bank

Internet users: 28.4% of the population (2011) World Bank

Take a closer look at Cuba

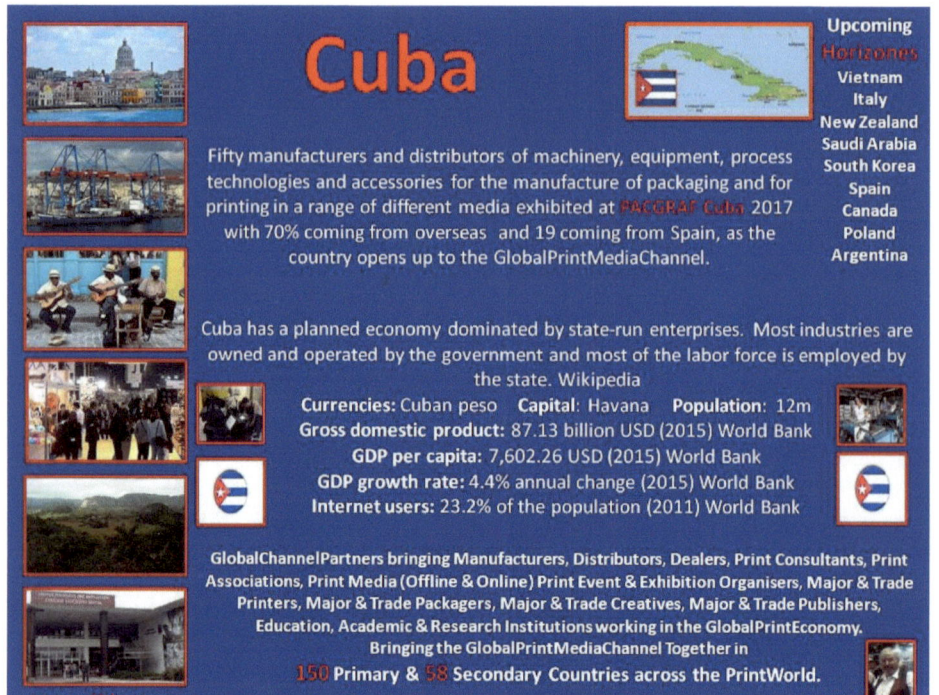

Take a look at (TALAT 30) Cuba

Fifty manufacturers and distributors of machinery, equipment, process technologies and accessories for the manufacture of packaging and for printing in a range of different media exhibited at **PACGRAF Cuba** 2017 with 70% coming from overseas and 19 coming from Spain, as the country opens up to the GlobalPrintMediaChannel.

Cuba has a planned economy dominated by state-run enterprises. Most industries are owned and operated by the government and most of the labor force is employed by the state. Wikipedia

Currencies: Cuban peso   Capital: Havana   Population: 12m
Gross domestic product: 87.13 billion USD (2015) World Bank
GDP per capita: 7,602.26 USD (2015) World Bank
GDP growth rate: 4.4% annual change (2015) World Bank
Internet users: 23.2% of the population (2011) World Bank

Take a closer look at Vietnam

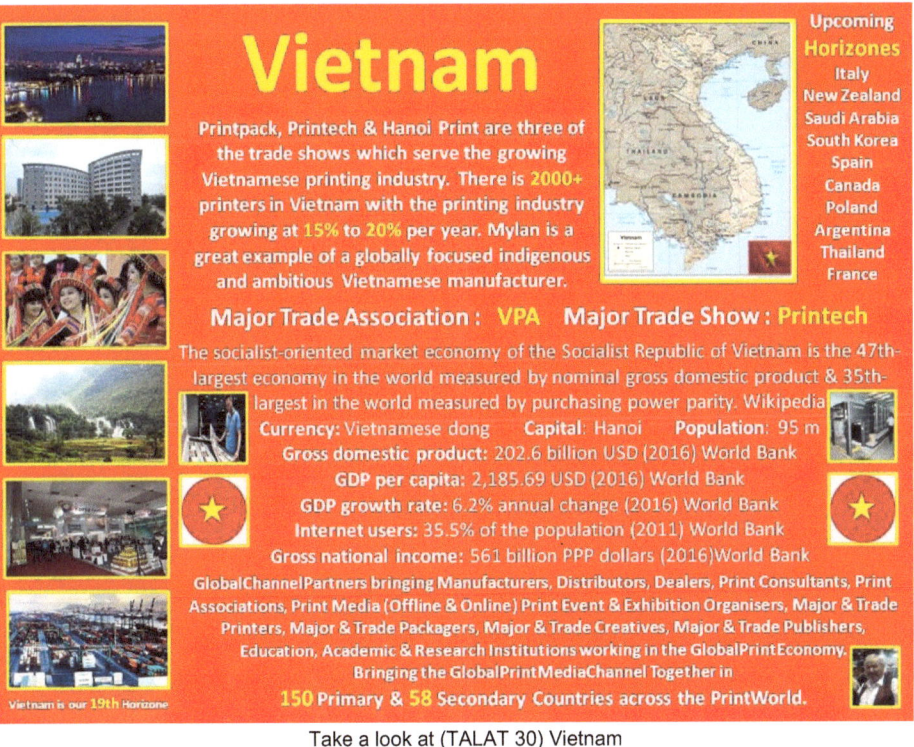

Take a look at (TALAT 30) Vietnam

Vietnam Printpack, Printech & Hanoi Print are three of the trade shows which serve the growing Vietnamese printing industry. There is 2000+ printers in Vietnam with the printing industry growing at 15% to 20% per year. Mylan is a great example of a globally focused indigenous and ambitious Vietnamese manufacturer.

Major Trade Association: VPA   Major Trade Show: Printech

The socialist-oriented market economy of the Socialist Republic of Vietnam is the 47th-largest economy in the world measured by nominal gross domestic product & 35th-largest in the world measured by purchasing power parity. Wikipedia

Currency: Vietnamese dong   Capital: Hanoi   Population: 95 m

Gross domestic product: 202.6 billion USD (2016) World Bank

GDP per capita: 2,185.69 USD (2016) World Bank

GDP growth rate: 6.2% annual change (2016) World Bank

Internet users: 35.5% of the population (2011) World Bank

Gross national income: 561 billion PPP dollars (2016) World Bank

Take a closer look at Italy

Take a look at (TALAT 30) Italy

Italy is one of the largest print production economies & also one of the most active & leading print manufacturers with companies such as the emerging APR Solutions & well established brands such as OMET, Petratto, Re & Sitma focusing on packaging (70%) & printing machinery (20%).

Major Trade Association: Acimga   Major Trade Show: Print4All

The economy of Italy is the 3rd-largest national economy in the euro zone, the 8th-largest by nominal GDP in the world, and the 12th-largest by GDP. Wikipedia

Currency: Euro   Capital: Rome   Population: 62m

Gross domestic product: 1.85 trillion USD (2016) World Bank

Government debt: 132.0% of GDP (2016) Eurostat

Unemployment rate: 10.9% (Feb 2018) Eurostat

GDP per capita: 30,527.27 USD (2016) World Bank

GDP growth rate: 0.9% annual changes (2016) World Bank

Gross national income: 2.317 trillion PPP dollars (2016) World Back

Take a closer look at New Zealand

Take a look at (TALAT 30) New Zealand

New Zealand 'WePrint' has just taken place as it looked to provide a forum for production people to exchange ideas and information about the printing process at the grass roots level. Going a step further and opening it up to all printers including digital & sheet fed and making it a New Zealand wide printing industry conference.

Major Trade Association: PrintNZ   Major Trade Magazine: NZP

The economy of New Zealand is the 53rd-largest national economy in the world when measured by nominal gross domestic product and the 68th-largest in the world when measured by purchasing power parity. Wikipedia
Currency: New Zealand dollar   Capital: Wellington Population: 5m
Gross domestic product: 185 billion USD (2016) World Bank
Exports: NZ$61.722 billion (FY 2013)

Take a closer look at Saudi Arabia

Take a look at (TALAT 30) Saudi Arabia

Saudi Arabia's printing industry is the third largest in the Arab world, following Lebanon & Egypt & is worth approximately USD $800 million. The printing sector continues to record an average annual growth rate of more than 8%. The printing sector's value in the region as a whole is expected to surpass USD $20 Billion

Major Trade Exhibition: Saudi Print & Pack 2019

The economy of Saudi Arabia is dependent on oil and has strong government control over major economic activities. The Saudi economy is the largest in the Arab world.

Currency: Saudi riyal   Capital: Riyadh   Population: 33 m

Gross domestic product: 646.4 billion USD (2016) World Bank

GDP per capita: 20,028.65 USD (2016) World Bank

GDP growth rate: 1.7% annual change (2016) World Bank

GNI per capita: 55,760 PPP dollars (2016) World Bank

Gross national income: 1.8 trillion PPP dollars (2016) World Bank

Internet users: 47.5% of the population (2011) World Bank

Take a closer look at South Korea

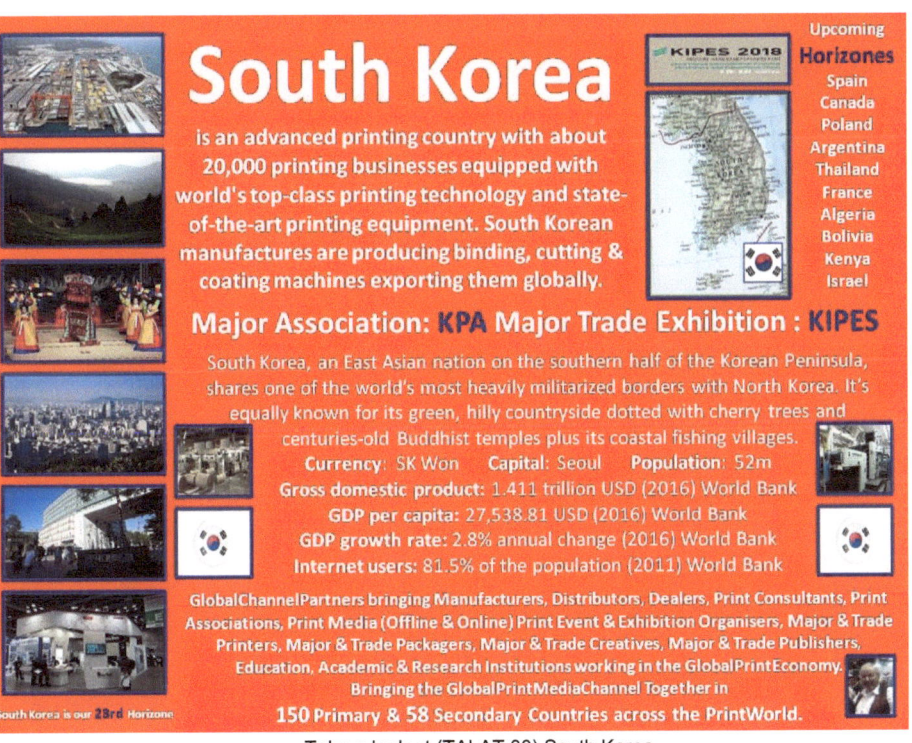

Take a look at (TALAT 30) South Korea

is an advanced printing country with about 20,000 printing businesses equipped with world's top-class printing technology and state-of-the-art printing equipment. South Korean manufactures are producing binding, cutting & coating machines exporting them globally.

Major Association: KPA Major Trade Exhibition: KIPES

South Korea, an East Asian nation on the southern half of the Korean Peninsula, shares one of the world's most heavily militarized borders with North Korea. It's equally known for its green, hilly countryside dotted with cherry trees and centuries-old Buddhist temples plus its coastal fishing villages.

Currency: SK Won   Capital: Seoul   Population: 52m

Gross domestic product: 1.411 trillion USD (2016) World Bank

GDP per capita: 27,538.81 USD (2016) World Bank

GDP growth rate: 2.8% annual change (2016) World Bank

Internet users: 81.5% of the population (2011) World Bank

Take a closer look at Spain

Take a look at (TALAT 30) Spain

is the 6th largest printing and packaging industry in the EU with some major international manufacturers with global reach incl Comexi, Ipagsa, Rotatek & Tauler. Also with some great distributor/dealers such as Abezeta, DHP, EMG, Envol Graphics, MKM, OPQ, Nuenka, SFS and TMZ. Barcelona hosts a great show every two years - Graphispag.

Major Association: FEIGRAF   Major Trade Exhibition: Graphispag

The economy of Spain is the world's fourteenth-largest by nominal GDP, and it is also one of the largest in the world by purchasing power parity. Wikipedia

Currency: Euro   Capital: Madrid   Population: 48m

Unemployment rate: 16.1% (Feb 2018) Eurostat

Gross domestic product: 1.232 trillion USD (2016) World Bank

Minimum wage: 858.55 EUR per month (Jan 2018) Eurostat

GDP per capita: 26,528.49 USD (2016) World Bank

GDP growth rate: 3.2% annual change (2016) World Bank

Take a closer look at Canada

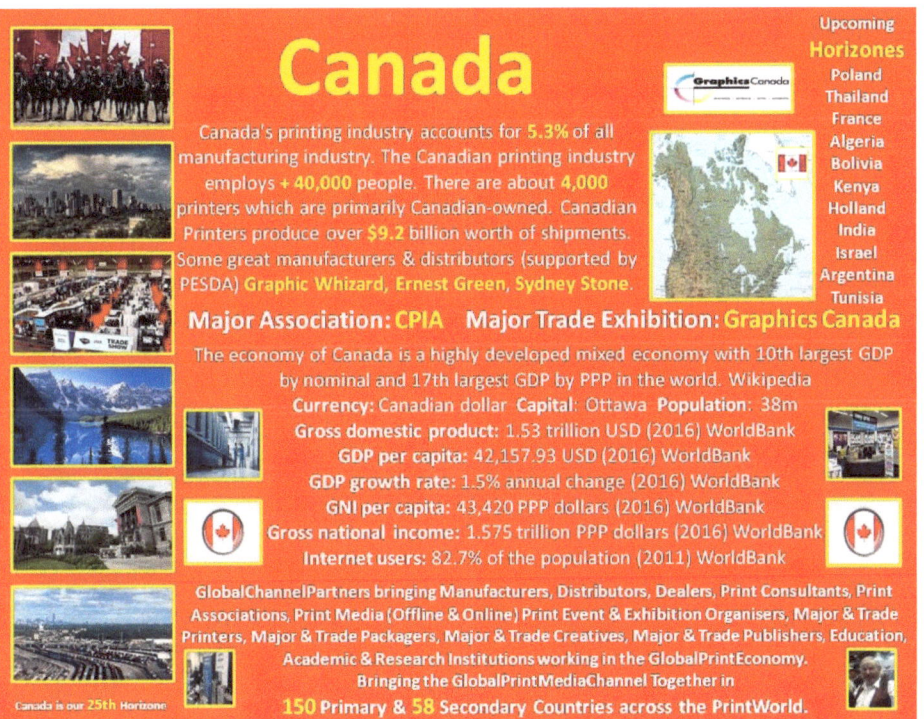

Take a look at (TALAT 30) Canada

Canada's printing industry accounts for 5.3% of all manufacturing industry. The Canadian printing industry employs + 40,000 people. There are about 4,000 printers which are primarily Canadian-owned. Canadian Printers produce over $9.2 billion worth of shipments. Some great manufacturers & distributors (supported by PESDA) Graphic Whizard, Ernest Green, Sydney Stone.

Major Association: CPIA   Major Trade Exhibition: Graphics Canada.

The economy of Canada is a highly developed mixed economy with 10th largest GDP by nominal and 17th largest GDP by PPP in the world. Currency: Canadian dollar. Capital: Ottawa Population: 38mGross domestic product: 1.53 trillion USD (2016) GDP per capita: 42,157.93 USD (2016) GDP growth rate: 1.5% annual change (2016) GNI per capita: 43,420 PPP dollars (2016) Gross national income: 1.575 trillion PPP dollars (2016)

Take a closer look at Poland

Take a look at (TALAT 30) Poland

Printing industry remains one of the fastest growing manufacturing industries in Poland generated by 8,600 companies employing more than 46,000 people with as many as 71% selling to the foreign markets. With 64% selling their products to Germany followed by France & the Netherlands (20%) & U.K. (17%). Some great manufacturers & dealers i.e. 123CTP & Akonda Major Association: Polska Izba Druka   Major Trade Exhibition: Poligrafia. The economy of Poland is the eighth largest economy in the European Union and the largest among the former Eastern Bloc members of the European Union.

Currency: Polish złoty   Capital: Warsaw   Population: 39m

Gross domestic product: 469.5 billion USD (2016)

GDP per capita: 12,372.42 USD (2016)

Minimum wage: 502.75 EUR per month (Jan 2018)

Unemployment rate: 4.4% (Nov 2017)

GDP growth rate: 2.7% annual change (2016)

GNI per capita: 26,770 PPP dollars (2016)

Take a closer look at Thailand

Take a look at (TALAT 30) Thailand

There are about 5,000 printing and packaging companies in Thailand employing in the order of 120,000 people, their collective output is valued at about $4.0bn with just under 2.0bn being exported mostly to ASEAN Economic Community; which has in the region of 600m Print Consumers. Printing in Thailand dates back to 1831 with a UK made press.

Major Association: TPA & FTPA   Major Trade Exhibition: PRINTECH

Thailand is a newly industrialized country. Its economy is heavily export-dependent, with exports accounting for more than two-thirds of its gross domestic product.

Currency: Thai baht   Capital: Bangkok P   Population: 70m
Gross domestic product: 406.8 billion USD (2016) WorldBank
GDP per capita: 5,907.91 USD (2016) WorldBank
GDP growth rate: 3.2% annual change (2016) WorldBank
GNI per capita: 16,070 PPP dollars (2016) WorldBank
Gross national income: 1.107 trillion PPP dollars (2016) WorldBank
Internet users: 23.7% of the population (2011) WorldBank

Take a closer look at France

Take a look at (TALAT 30) France

France is the 3rd largest printing industry in Europe (EU & RoE) and the 7th in the PrintWorld. MGi is an examples of French manufacturers. Brise, Clementz Euromegras Matrel, RBS & Siproudhis as distributors & have been serving the French market for many years.

Major Association: Symop Major Trade Exhibition: Graphitec

France has the world's 7th largest economy by 2017 nominal figures and the 10th largest economy by PPP figures. It has the 3rd largest economy in the European Union after Germany and the United Kingdom. Wikipedia

Currencies: Euro, CFP franc Capital: Paris Population: 68m

Gross domestic product: 2.465 trillion USD (2016) World Bank

Unemployment rate: 8.9% (Feb 2018) Eurostat

GDP per capita: 36,854.97 USD (2016) World Bank

Minimum wage: 1,498.47 EUR per month (Jan 2018) Eurostat

Government debt: 96.5% of GDP (2016) Eurostat

GDP growth rate: 1.2% annual change (2016) World Bank

Take a closer look at Algeria

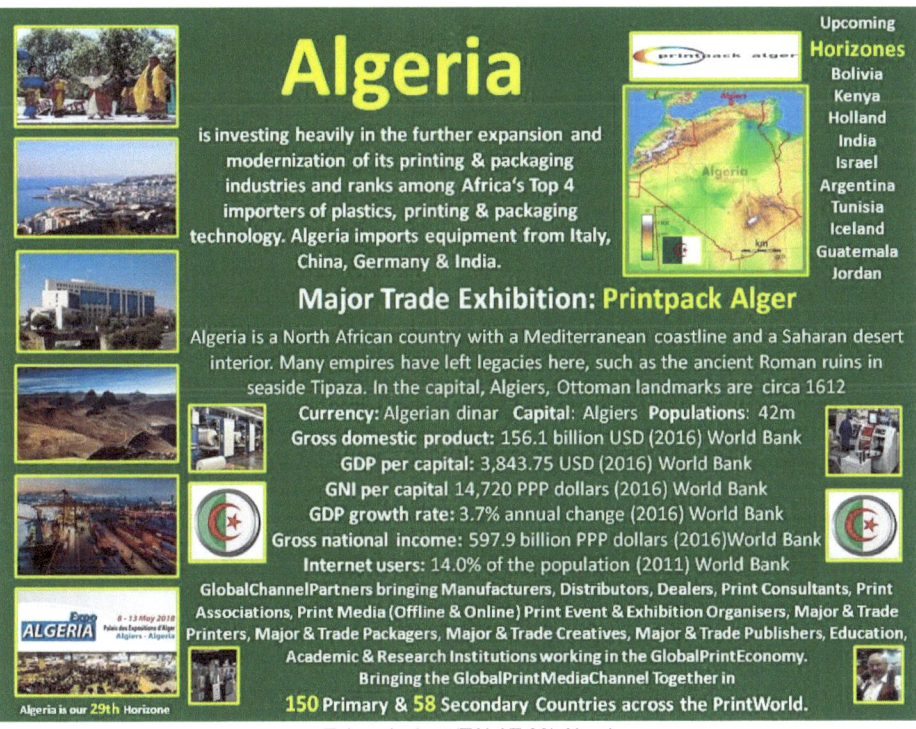

Take a look at (TALAT 30) Algeria

is investing heavily in the further expansion and modernization of its printing & packaging industries and ranks among Africa's Top 4 importers of plastics, printing & packaging technology. Algeria imports equipment from Italy, China, Germany & India. Major Trade Exhibition: Printpack Alger

Algeria is a North African country with a Mediterranean coastline and a Saharan desert interior. Many empires have left legacies here, such as the ancient Roman ruins in seaside Tipaza. In the capital, Algiers, Ottoman landmarks are circa 1612

Currency: Algerian dinar   Capital: Algiers Populations: 42m

Gross domestic product: 156.1 billion USD (2016) World Bank

GDP per capital: 3,843.75 USD (2016) World Bank

GNI per capital 14,720 PPP dollars (2016) World Bank

GDP growth rate: 3.7% annual change (2016) World Bank

Gross national income: 597.9 billion PPP dollars (2016) World Bank

Internet users: 14.0% of the population (2011) World Bank

Take a closer look at Bolivia

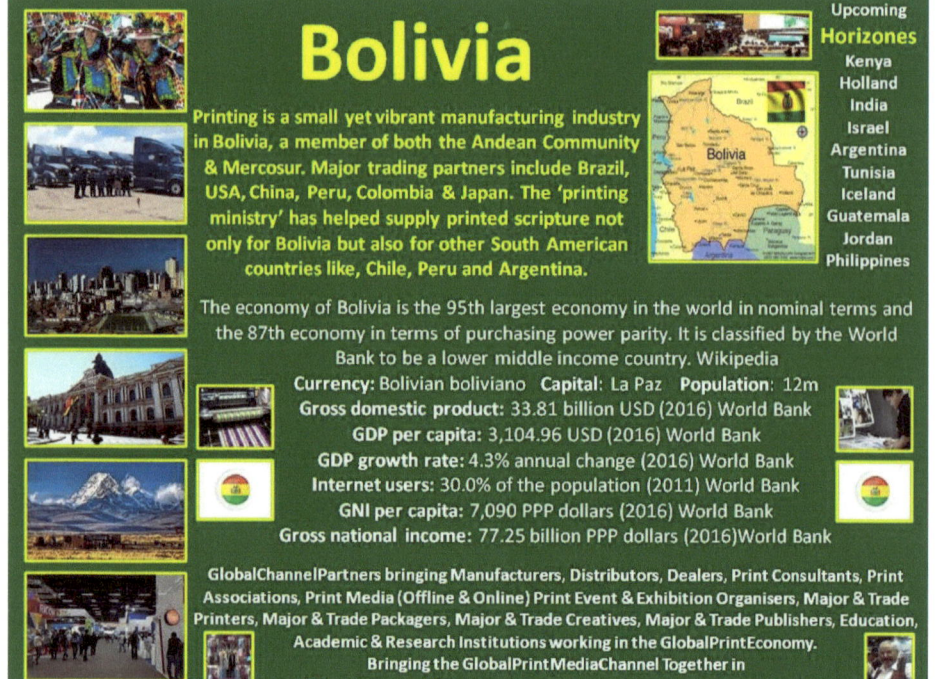

Take a look at (TALAT 30) Bolivia

Printing is a small yet vibrant manufacturing industry in Bolivia, a member of both the Andean Community & Mercosur. Major trading partners include Brazil, USA, China, Peru, Colombia & Japan. The 'printing ministry' has helped supply printed scripture not only for Bolivia but also for other South American countries like, Chile, Peru. The economy of Bolivia is the 95th largest economy in the world in nominal terms and the 87th economy in terms of purchasing power parity. It is classified by the World Bank to be a lower middle income country. Wikipedia

Currency: Bolivian boliviano   Capital: La Paz   Population: 12m

Gross domestic product: 33.81 billion USD (2016) World Bank

GDP per capita: 3,104.96 USD (2016) World Bank

GDP growth rate: 4.3% annual change (2016) World Bank

Internet users: 30.0% of the population (2011) World Bank

GNI per capita: 7,090 PPP dollars (2016) World Bank

Gross national income: 77.25 billion PPP dollars (2016) World Bank

BONUS CONTENT to TALAT 30

GlobalChannelPartners 2016
'The Future of the Channel'

'The State of the Channel'	1 - 10
'The Purpose of the Channel'	11 - 20
'The Players in the Channel'	21 - 30
'Some Members of the Channel'	31 - 40
'The Future of the Channel'	41 - 50

 Created & Presented By Danny Moloney

Take a look at (TALAT 30) Image Description Channel Perspectives

'The Future of the Channel - An Introduction' is preceded by others modules in this series which cover, the State, the purpose, the players, some members and here the future of the Channel; all soon to be released.

In 'The State of the Channel', we covered (as per the slides below), the conventional relationship between the channel partners specifically of manufacturers, distributors/dealers and the market (represented by printers). In addition, we looked at the life cycles in terms of the manufacturers the distributors/dealers and the market i.e printer) (more in the GlobalChannelPartners 101 – Channel Overview).

It can be seen here that the conventional progress is manufacturers leading, distributor / dealers interfacing between the manufacturer and market (printer) and tracking the market to best represent their needs to the manufacturers.

It can also very graphically be seen that the manufacturer in PINK made good headway but then fell back, the distributor / dealer in ORANGE fell back even more sharply but the Printer in GREEN has due to technological imperatives seen his/her curve progress ever up wards mainly at the cost of conventional channel partners.

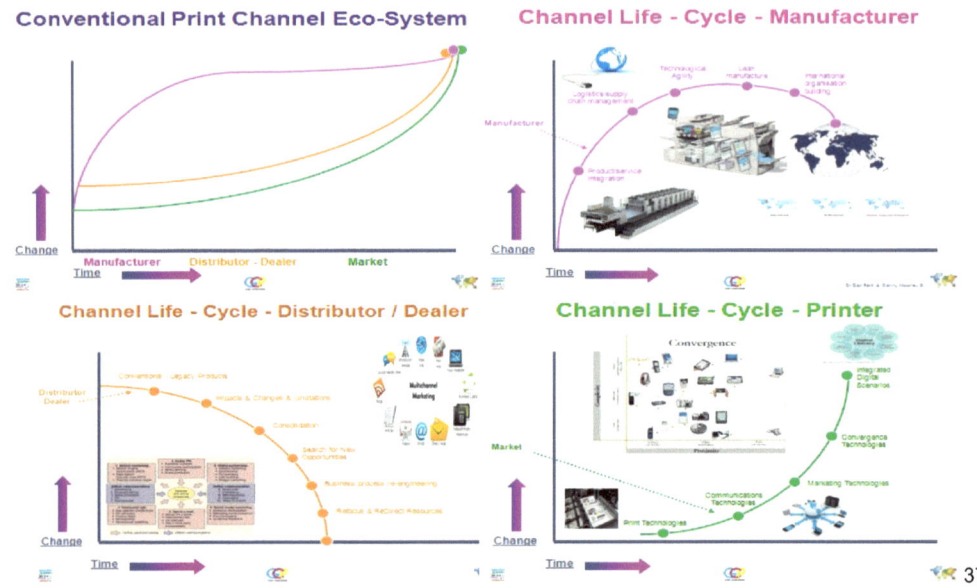

Take a look at (TALAT 30) Image Description The Paradigm

All of which demonstrates that not only the production of print has been redefined but also the supply chain that serves it i.e. the Channel has had to change with the 'times'.

Looking towards what do we consider constitutes the GlobalPrintMediaChannel in the future? We propose that manufacturers, distributors, dealers, consultants, associations, printmedia, events and exhibitions, education, academic and research institutions form the GlobalPrintMediaChannel in so far as they play varying roles in the success of the process; we can take each on in turn (more in the GlobalChannelPartners 101 – Channel Overview) briefly here as part of our future view;

The GlobalPrintMediaChannel

- 1. Manufacturers
- 2. Distributors
- 3. Dealers
- 4. Major & Trade Printers
- 5. Associations
- 6. Consultants
- 7. Media
- 8. Events & Exhibitions
- 9. Education
- 10. Academic & Research Institutions

Serves the Printer

Take a look at (TALAT 30) Image Description Serving the Printer

First of all, it is worth stating once again that the purpose of the channel is to serve the market specifically the printer and that the members of the GlobalPrintMediaChannel play a vital part in this process.

Manufacturers: have been used to developing, creating and manufacturing the products and services which the printing industry uses as print producers. In the future, they will need to be more inventive, creative and innovative in order to satisfy both the changing demands but also the emerging needs of the global print market.

Distributors: buy and market the products and the services from the manufacturers which the printing industry uses as print producers ordinarily to dealers.

Dealers: buy and market the products and the services from the manufacturers and or the distributors which the printing industry uses as print producers ordinarily to printers.

Consultants: assist and support all other members of the GlobalPrintMediaChannel and to provide and promote their collective efforts to the printing industry with a focus on consultancy.

Associations: assist and support all of the other members of the GlobalPrintMediaChannel and to provide and promote their collective efforts to the printing industry with a focus on association benefits.

PrintMedia: assist and support all of the other members of the GlobalPrintMediaChannel and to provide and promote their collective efforts to the printing industry with a focus on providing insight in to our industry.

Events: assist and support all of the other members of the GlobalPrintMediaChannel and to provide and promote their collective efforts to the printing industry with a focus on providing events for our industry.

Exhibitions: assist and support all of the other members of the GlobalPrintMediaChannel and to provide and promote their collective efforts to the printing industry with a focus on providing exhibitions for our industry.

Education: assist and support all of the other members of the GlobalPrintMediaChannel and to provide and promote their collective efforts to the printing industry providing education for our industry.

Academic: assist and support all of the other members of the GlobalPrintMediaChannel and to provide and promote their collective efforts to the printing industry providing academic resource for our industry.

Research Institutions: assist and support all of the other members of the GlobalPrintMediaChannel and to provide and promote their collective efforts to the printing industry providing research into our industry.

Below is a diagram of the conventional print media channel. Where the Manufacturer (in PINK) leads on both the time and the change axis by creating the products and services which the channel (including the print producers) can then use effectively and profitably.

The Distributor (staying closer to the manufacturer and working together with the dealer, the dealer working more closely with the market i.e. print producers (both on ORANGE) produce the dynamic of representing the manufacturer to the market.

The Market (representing the print producer) is led by the channel (representing by the combined manufactures, distributor and dealer channel partners (in GREEN) and feeding back to the channel what products they feel they need, could use or would benefit from having supplied to them.

'The Channel of the Future'

PRINT

Purposed
Relevant
Innovative
Necessary
Transcendent

150 Primary Countries & 58 Secondary Countries

Take a look at (TALAT 30) Image Description PRINT A Definition

The Conventional channel described above has been influenced by the following (more in the GlobalChannelPartners 101 – Channel Overview) market and technological impacts;

Legacy & Proximity Relationships: whereby the manufacturers needed the channel partners to take products to the market and receiving information and feedback on the market.

Structural & Economic & Technological Change: significantly in business process & practice.

Market Distribution 'Opportunities' with **Product & Marketing Margins**: the duality of the exchange between manufacturer and their distribution partners, now in constant change.

Universal 'Accessible Distribution and Logistics: the great catalyst of change in our channel.

Virtual everything, everywhere all the time: the new and dynamic paradigm in our channel.

Emerging Economics of Applied Knowledge: the core of our program and the scenarios we are building to support the channel into the future.

'The Channel of the Future'

Multi - Year, Original GlobalPrintMediaChannel Research Program

An unique exploration of GlobalPrintMediaChannel dynamics

Understand the extent, value and purpose of the GlobalPrintMediaChannel

Develop a comprehensive dataset for the GlobalPrintMediaChannel

Predict the future 'form, shape and purpose' of the GlobalPrintMediaChannel

Produce and publish a definitive 'GlobalPrintMediaChannel'@ Print17

Bringing the GlobalPrintMediaChannel - Together

Take a look at (TALAT 30) Image Description The Channel of the Future

The Channel Life – Cycle - Manufacturer (more in the GlobalChannelPartners 101 – Channel Overview) can be briefly but not exhaustively described as follows;

The manufacturer has the responsibility to create the products and services which initiate the Channel Process. A selection of the recent economic and technology influences and trends which guide their approach include product service integration, logistic / supply chain management, technological agility, lean manufacturer and international organisation building; these and many other impacts have put manufacturers into a constant state of apprehension.

It can be seen by the shape of the graph below that manufacturers have in many cases been losing the fight to stay ahead of the trends that have impacting on them over the last 20 years and many have gone out of business and many more have entered our industry from areas outside of traditional printing; as can been seen by the changes in the exhibitor population of Graph Expo - Chicago between 1993 and 2015.

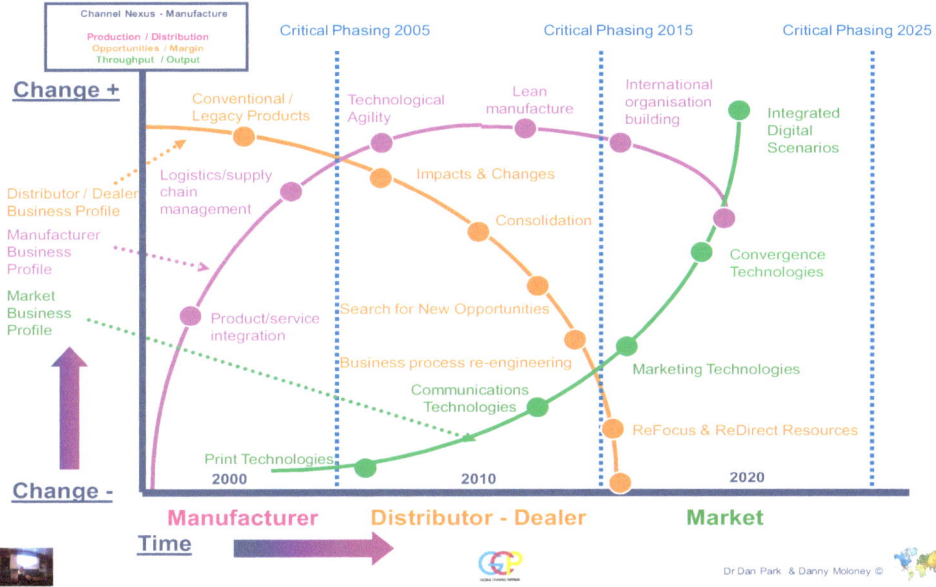

Take a look at (TALAT 30) Image Description Strategy Scenario One – 2015

The Channel Life - Cycle - Distributor/Dealer (more in the GlobalChannelPartners 101 – Channel Overview) can be briefly but not exhaustively described as follows; conventional legacy products, impacts change and limitations, consolidation, search for new opportunities, business process engineering and refocus and redirect resources. Dealer having become used to a settled business and technological environment in the 1960s to the early 90s and have struggled valiantly to stay abreast of the changes affecting them on both sides of their business base. Constant changes in products, services and client demands have taken their toll on available and legacy knowledge the dealer had previously relied upon and which today is in a permanent state of flux.

Distributor and Dealers all across the print world have sought to maintain and regain relevance to the channel i.e. as the intermediary between the manufacturer and the print (the market). As the graph below suggests, dealers have been losing the fight to stay in the game which is why so many have gone out of business across the print world and why so many more are striving to find new purpose and to add new value to their role.

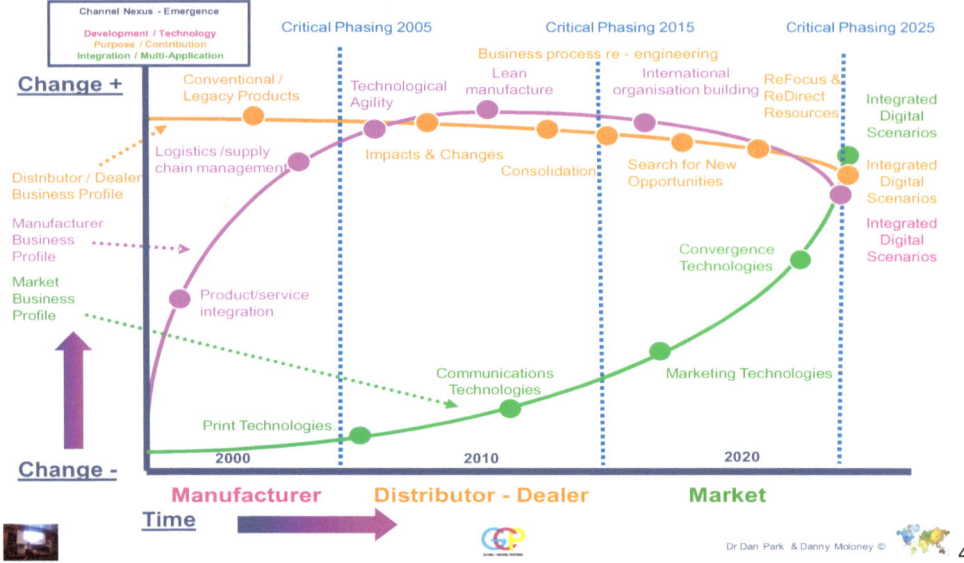

Take a look at (TALAT 30) Image Description Strategy Scenario Two – 2020

The Channel Life - Cycle - Printer (more in the GlobalChannelPartners 101 – Channel Overview) can be briefly but not exhaustively described as follows; print technologies, communications technologies, marketing technologies, convergence technologies and integrated digital scenarios.

Just as the manufacturer, distributor and dealer have been struggling to stay abreast with the market, the printer equally has been inundated by a tsunami of new and mostly innovative print production methods, many of which have left conventional and even digital print behind.

The effect on the printer has primarily been one of managing production change and as a corollary the expectations of the market. The way and the why of print is changing. What we need print for 20 years ago is not what we need it for today (in many cases) witness business forms. Print was once a standalone function necessary for all forms of communication, transactions and marketing functions. Today, print is being increasingly integrated into the mainstream of data and information flow.

These changes require different forms of printer both in terms of personnel, management and equipment. The channel still has a role and purpose in providing both for these changes and for these needs.

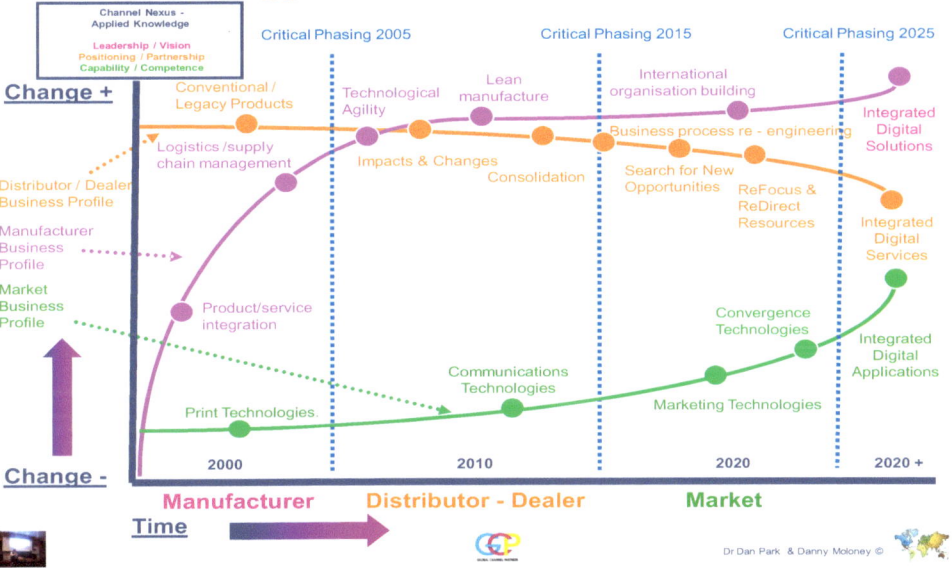

Take a look at (TALAT 30) Image Description Strategy Scenario Three 2025

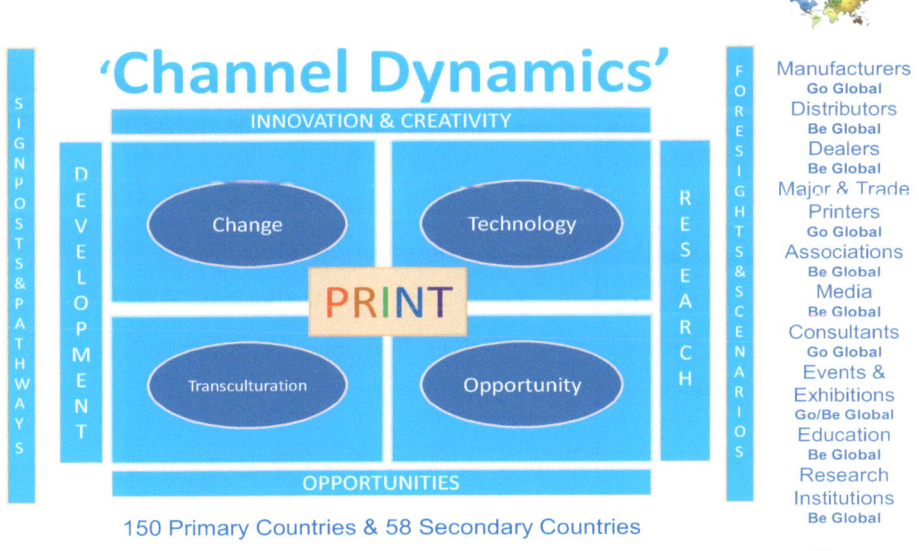

Take a look at (TALAT 30) Image Description Channel Dynamics

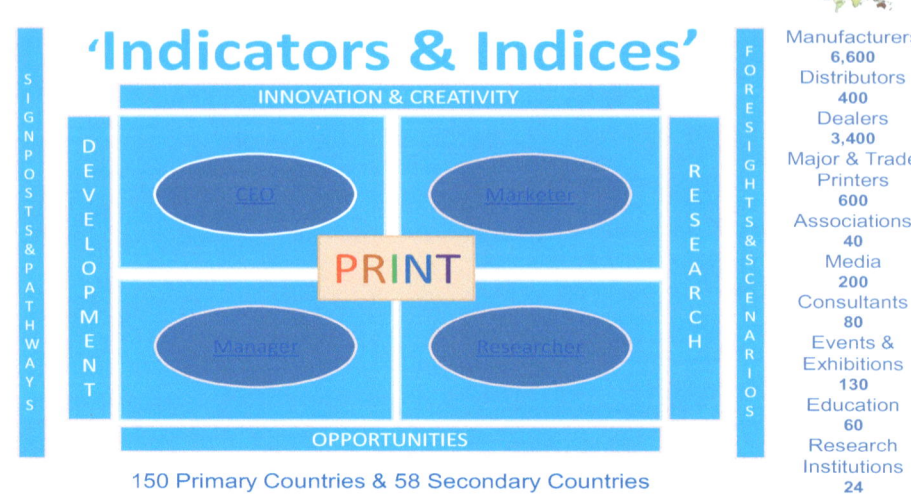

Take a look at (TALAT 30) Image Description Indicators & Indices

In summary, it is clear that the channel has and is changing and in many respects the channel is not prepared to manage the process going forward. With the average age of the archetypal printer being in their late 40s and the average age of the new knowledge consumer (print is a knowledge transfer mechanism) being in the mid 20s. In addition the role of PRINT is being redesigned almost on a daily basis (our new acronym for the role and purpose of PRINT is contained in our 'The Future of the Channel' e-book which follows shortly.

Print remains one of the largest industries in the world and has accumulated hundreds of years of legacy value and communication relevance, There are thousands of people working in the GlobalPrintMediaChannel with that amount of creativity and inventiveness we are assured of a strong and successful future for the channel.

We invite you to stay with us as new programs come on line which will help us all to navigate both the changes and the contours of the emerging and ever changing GlobalPrintMediaChannel. Our next e-book in this series is 'The Purpose of the Channel' followed by 'The Players in the Channel', then 'Some Members of the Channel'; and finally 'The Future of the Channel; will help us to do navigate the best route ahead.

Take a look at (TALAT 30) Image Description the GlobalChannelPartners Summit 2018 - Manchester

In PIcture Gram (1) immediately above, we outline (descriptions will follow in future editions)

GlobalChannelPartners Summit 2018 - Manchester

Summit - Expo - Forum - Programs - Research

'Printing - The Original Creative Industry'

Strategy - Growth - Innovation - Leadership - Profitability - Alliances - Scenarios - Technology

Friday 30th November EXTENDED day 8.00 am to 10.00 pm

Take a look at (TALAT 30) Image Description the GlobalChannelPartnersPavilion

In PictureGram (2) immediately above, we outline (descriptions will follow in future editions) our now typically Global Channel Partners Pavilion and Print Trade shows around the Print World.

GlobalChannelPavilions creates New Business - New Markets - New Opportunities - New Insights - New Perspectives - New Relationships by Going Global in North America, South America, Europe, Africa, The Middle East, Asia & Austral/Asia, GlobalChannelPartners 'Bringing the GlobalPrintMediaChannel Together'

Take a look at (TALAT 30) Image Description GlobalChannelPartners Champions across the PrintWorld

In Picture Gram (3) immediately above, we outline (descriptions will follow in future editions) and show some of our Global Channel Champions receiving their now annual awards which always take place at what was previously as GASC Event and is now an APTech Event. Featured in the picture are LinoMatic, Tim Murphy of PrintWare, Presstek, Chris Manley of Graphco, John, Linda & Jeff McCusker of Dotworks, Michael B. Frawley of MCT Digital, CRON, Alan Oppenheim of Morgana, Rick Principato of Tower Products, Matt of Trimatt, Gary Murphy of Merlin Press Parts, Dennis Mason of Mason Consulting, Roger & Brett Giza of Burnishine Products, David Steinhardt of Idealliance, Ike Savitt of Gate Group, Jack Noonan of MGi, Max Dunn & Chris Jacobson of Silicon Publishing, Mike Fichera & Pat Leavitt of Dealer Communicator and Saul Spiel & Frank Bagrosky of Spiel Associates.

Take a look at (TALAT 30) Image Description GlobalChannelPartners across the Academic PrintWorld

In Picture Gram (4) immediately above, we outline (descriptions will follow in future editions) we outline of academic credentials upon which our 'Practice Led – Theory Based' philosophy is based and we outline our academic credentials and research interests.

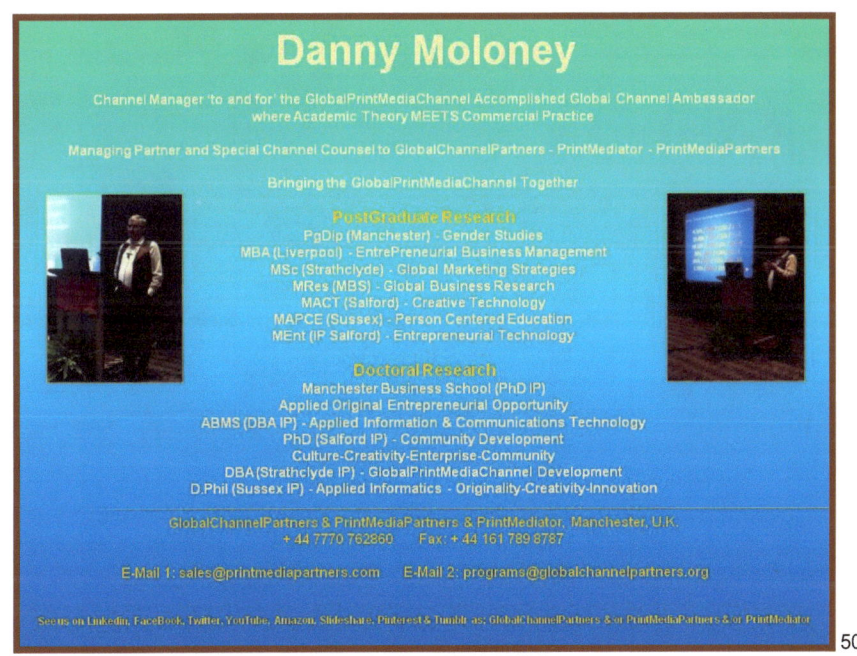

Take a look at (TALAT 30)
Image Description Core Academic Profile, Interests, Research Areas and Credentials.

In PictureGram (5) immediately above, we outline (descriptions will follow in future editions) our core academic profile, interests, research areas and credentials upon which our 'Practice Led – Theory Based' philosophy is based. Our SEVEN areas are as follows **Homigenesis** (Each Person has their own unique Personal Growth & Development Opportunities) - **TechnoPreneur** (using ICT to develop opportunity) - **Originateur** (creating the idea before the idea) - **Hominist** (Acknowledging & Championing the Male Perspective) - **Ecclesiast** (using community, creativity, enterprise and culture to enhance the 'place' where you were born, live or work) - **Individuateur** (Building Capacity - Capability - Competence - Opportunity) & **PrintMediateur** (developing the GlobalPrintMedia channel).

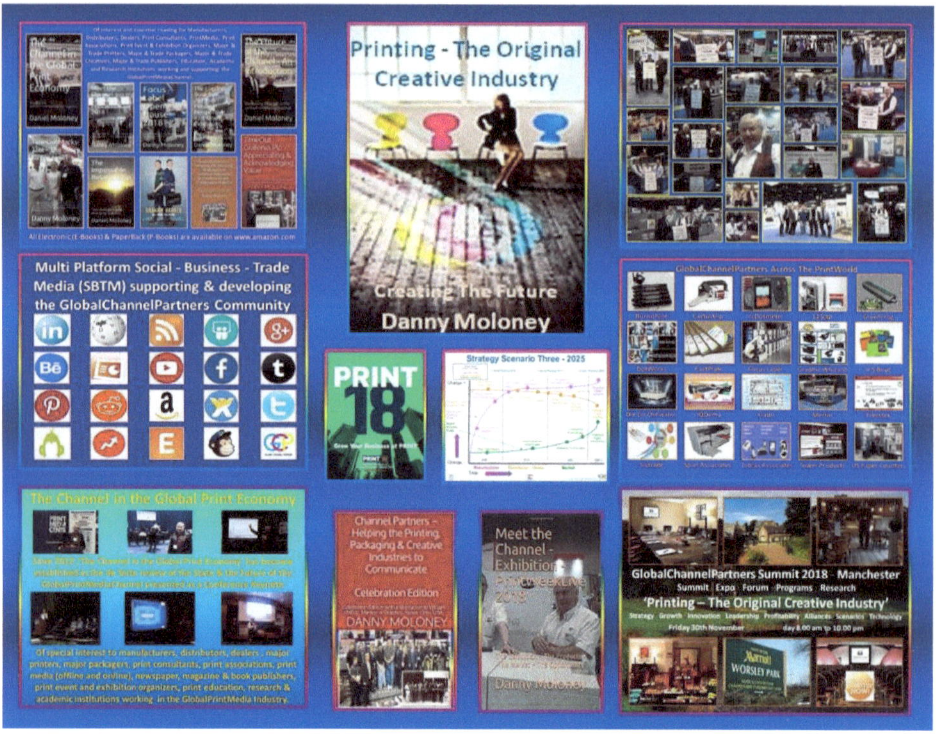

51

Take a look at (TALAT 30) Image Description PrintMediaPartners Products

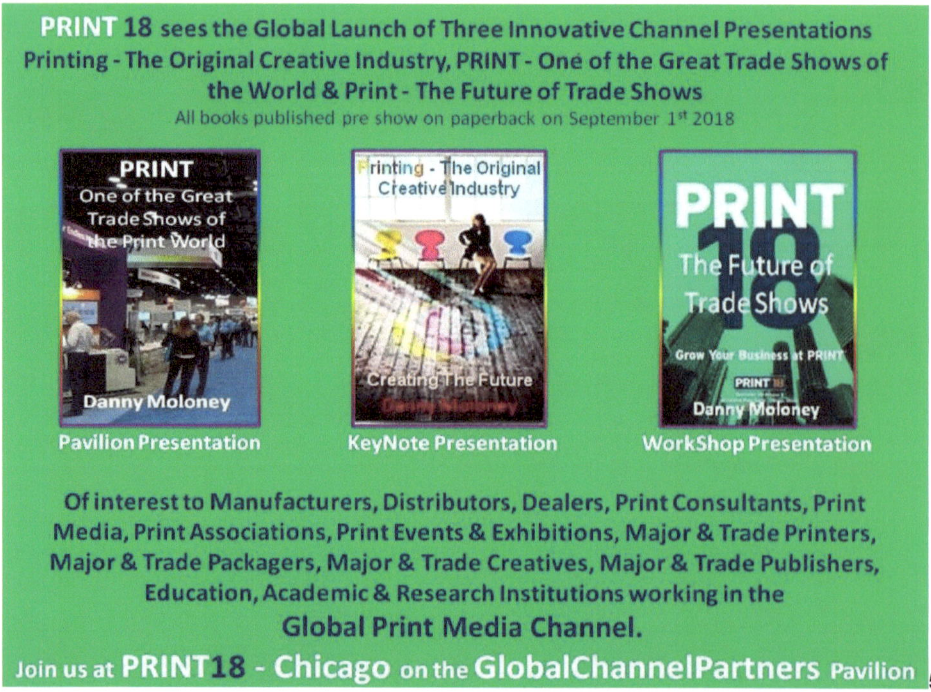

52

Take a look at (TALAT 30) Image Description PRINT 2018

PrintWorld

Afghanistan, Albania, Algeria, Andorra, Angola, Anguilla, Antigua Barbuda, Argentina, Armenia, Australia, Austria, Azerbaijan, Bahamas, Bahrain, Bangladesh, Barbados, Belarus, Belgium, Belize, Benin, Bermuda, Bhutan, Bolivia, Bosnia & Herzegovina, Botswana, Brazil, Brunei Darussalam, Bulgaria, Burkina Faso, Myanmar/Burma, Burundi, Cambodia, Cameroon, Canada, Cape Verde, Cayman Islands, Central African Republic, Chad, Chile, China, Colombia, Comoros, Congo, Costa Rica, Croatia, Cuba, Cyprus, Czech Republic, Democratic Republic of the Congo, Denmark, Djibouti, Dominica, Dominican Republic, Ecuador, Egypt, El Salvador, Equatorial Guinea, Eritrea, Estonia, Ethiopia, Fiji, Finland, France, French Guiana, Gabon, Gambia, Georgia, Germany, Ghana, Great Britain, Greece, Grenada, Guadeloupe, Guatemala, Guinea, Guinea-Bissau, Guyana, Haiti, Honduras, Hungary, Iceland, India, Indonesia, Iran, Iraq, Ireland, Israel, Italy, Ivory Coast (Cote d'Ivoire), Jamaica, Japan, Jordan, Kazakhstan, Kenya, Kosovo, Kuwait, Kyrgyzstan, Laos, Latvia, Lebanon, Lesotho, Liberia, Libya, Liechtenstein, Lithuania, Luxembourg, Macedonia, Madagascar, Malawi, Malaysia, Maldives, Mali, Malta, Martinique, Mauritania, Mauritius, Mayotte, Mexico, Moldova, Monaco, Mongolia, Montenegro, Montserrat, Morocco, Mozambique, Namibia, Nepal, Netherlands, New Zealand, Nicaragua, Niger, Nigeria, North Korea, Norway, Oman, Pacific Islands, Pakistan, Panama, Papua New Guinea, Paraguay, Peru, Philippines, Poland, Portugal, Puerto Rico, Qatar, Reunion, Romania, Russia, Rwanda, Saint Kitts and Nevis, Saint Lucia, Saint Vincent's & Grenadines, Samoa, Sao Tome and Principe, Saudi Arabia, Senegal, Serbia, Seychelles, Sierra Leone, Singapore, Slovakia, Slovenia, Solomon Islands, Somalia, South Africa, South Korea, South Sudan, Spain, Sri Lanka, Sudan, Suriname, Swaziland, Sweden, Switzerland, Syria, Tajikistan, Tanzania, Thailand, Timor Leste, Togo, Trinidad & Tobago, Tunisia, Turkey, Turkmenistan, Turks & Caicos Islands, Uganda, Ukraine, United Arab Emirates United States of America (USA), Uruguay, Uzbekistan, Venezuela, Vietnam, Virgin Islands (UK), Virgin Islands (US), Yemen, Zambia, Zimbabwe.

Bringing the GlobalPrintMediaChannel Together ACROSS the PrintWorld

Take a look at (TALAT 30) Countries of the PRINTWorld

HomiGenesis Signature

Our six original content series include the following;

(HomiGenesis as part of CallMeHominist)
Covering the birth, nurturing and early growth of the unique
'Homigenesis - An Uniquely Individual Male Perspective' philosophy

Encompassing and developing the following key concepts;

Individual - Empathic - Gregarious - Thoughtful - Appreciative - Holistic

Presented & promoted via a combination of 1) academic research papers and specially created business, 2) Case studies, popular published **3)** e-books & **4)** p-books, 5) formal lectures, 6) informative seminars, 7) Knowledge exchange presentations, 8) keynote speeches and 9) consultancy & 10) coaching.

Hashtags
#**Homigenesis**,

#**ecclesiast**, #**hominist**, #**individuateur**, #**PrintMediateur**, #**TechnoPreneur** #**Originateur**,

Research Formats
Insights - Spotlights - Signposts - Pathways - Foresights - Scenarios - Opportunities

Jaeger (500)   Chronologs (2,000)   Genesis (5,000)
Essays (10,000)   Stories (20,000)   Novels & Theses (80,000)

Each containing an uniquely innovative 'Homigenesis Moment' for
Ecclesiast - Hominist - Individuateur - Originateur - PrintMediateur - TechnoPreneur

See also and keep in touch on
Ecclesiast: Acquiring & Developing Knowledge via Community-Culture-Creativity-EnterPrise
Hominist: Acquiring & Developing Knowledge via Masculinity-Man-Male-Manly-Manliness.
Individuateur: Acquiring & Developing Knowledge via Data-Information-Analysis-Knowledge
Originateur: Acquiring & Developing Knowledge via Originality-Lifelong Learning -Transculturation-Innovation
PrintMediateur: Acquiring & Developing Knowledge via Channel-Media-Marketing-Print
TechnoPreneur: Acquiring & Developing Knowledge via Capacity-Capability-Competence-Opportunity.

Take a look at (TALAT 30) GlobalHorizones

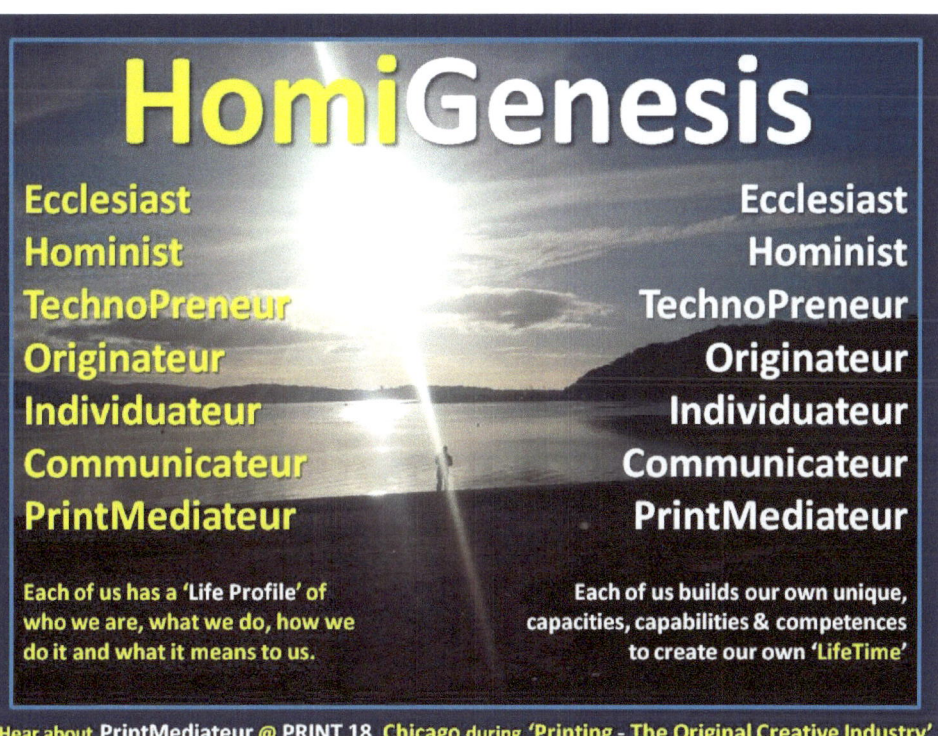

Take a look at (TALAT 30)- Homigenesis

Friday 20th July 2018

Thank you for reading

Take a look at (TALAT 30)

GlobalChannelPartners - PrintMediator - PrintMediateur - PrintMediaPartners
Part of GlobalMeHPTE, Greater Eccles, Manchester, United Kingdom.

Homigenesis
TechnoPreneur - Originateur - Hominist - Ecclesiast - Individuateur - Originateur
Tele: +44 7770 762860   Fax: + 44 161 789 8787
E-Mail: programs@globalchannelpartners.org

Words - 7,496   **Images - 54**   **Pages - 53**

www.ingramcontent.com/pod-product-compliance
Lightning Source LLC
Chambersburg PA
CBHW040329220526
45473CB00009B/2615